Country Talk

A Collection of American Country Colloquialisms

Diane Suchetka

Illustrated by Andrea Winton

Country Roads Press

Designed and produced by Sally Hill McMillan and Associates, Inc., Charlotte, North Carolina.

Published by Country Roads Press
P.O. Box 286, Lower Main Street
Castine, Maine 04421

Library of Congress Cataloging-in-Publication Data
Suchetka, Diane.
   Country talk : a collection of American country colloquialisms /
Diane Suchetka.
      p.   cm.
   ISBN 1-56626-029-9 : $12.95
   1. English language—United States—Terms and phrases.   2. English
language—Spoken English—United States.   3. Country life—United
States—Terminology.   4. Aphorisms and apothegms.   5. Figures of
speech.   6. Americanisms.   I. Title.
PE2839.S86   1993
427' .973—dc20   93-7942
                                                                         CIP

Printed in the United States of America.
10   9   8   7   6   5   4   3   2   1

To Alice, wherever you are, I kept my promise.

To Mom and Dad, I love you more than the
cat loves the cream jar.

And to Henry,
who really is hotter than Georgia asphalt.

Thanks to the following folks who contributed to this book:

Beebe Barksdale
Sheila Bennett
Charlie Bodine
Henry Boggan and his callers
Jamie Braswell
Randy Brazell
Jo Bremer
Jay Bridges
Patricia Brown
Tony Brown
Andrew Brunkala Sr.
Frank Brunkala Sr.
Nancy Budd
Chip Caine
Cheryl Carpenter
Johnny Carson
Maxine Chrosniak
Shay Clanton
Bill Clinton
Otis Dowdy
Deborah Dunn
Beth Ely
Scott Fair
Olen Foley
Trent Foley
Sarah Franquet
Tim Funk
Karen Garloch
Alison Gilbert
Henry Gilbert
Pete Gilbert
Kathie Gimla
Mike Gordon
Tom Gordon
John Grant
Pat Gubbins
Ann Doss Helms
Robin Hemley
Bruce Henderson
John Hooe
Joan Hope
Dan Huntley
Lynn Ischay
Justin Jaklic
Dwuan June
Deborah Jung
John Boy and Billy
Pam Kelley
David King
Jeri Fischer Krentz

Barb Leverone
Louise Lione
Gale Martin
Richard Maschal
Brooks Maxwell
John McBride
Kathleen McClain
Randy McDonald
Deb McLean
Mick McNeely
Harriet Melton
Mary Carol Michie
Barbara Miller
Michael Montgomery
Jane Murphy
Brenda Nance
Mary Newsom
Gary Nielson
Allen Norwood
Mark Oden
Louis Oppenheim
Tonya Wertz Orbaugh
Anne Pendergrast
Lolo Pendergrast
B.J. Perlmutt
David Perlmutt
Jerry Potter
Bill Pryor and the guys
   at Parnell-Martin
Kathi Purvis
Robert D. Raiford
Doug Robarchek
Jane Shoemaker
Tony Simpson
Mary Ellen Snodgrass
Tom Sorensen
Joe Sovacool
Michael Suchetka
Rosie Suchetka
Jim Teat Jr.
Lawrence Toppman
Sam Treadaway
Doak Turner
Scott Verner
Ralph Walker
Dot Reynolds Wilkinson
Jacki Winters
Jim Wrinn
Special thanks to Caroline Beyrau
and Sally Hill McMillan.

Country Talk

Table of Contents

Introduction

"He was sweatin' like a Christian Scientist with appendicitis."

"She's so fat it takes two men and a boy just to look at her."

"He can fix anything from a broken heart to the break of day."

Sayin's like that are to your ears what chicken fryin' on Sunday mornin' is to your nose.

Faster'n lightnin', they whisk you back to a better place, a simpler time. Kinda make you wonder how you got so far away from home.

Well, before it's too late, pull up a chair, read with us and remember back to the days when words of wisdom were funny too, when family was everything and money was nothin', when folks weren't too uppity to laugh at each other — and themselves. Remember back to the days when nobody would even think of callin' anybody else crazy. "Her cornbread ain't quite done in the middle," they'd say instead.

The clever insults and candid descriptions are an almost- lost art form that sprang from everyday life, not exotic experiences or faraway places. And they're as thrifty as the people who use them. With just a few words, they paint a picture or tell a story that makes you sigh or wince or chuckle. They are the poetry of the people.

The blank pages at the end of this book are there for you to add your own sayin's — the ones mama used, the ones that still slip out of your own mouth sometimes before you even realize it.

If you've a mind to, send 'em along to us so we can add them to the next edition of Country Talk.

We'd be mighty obliged, tickled pink, in cooter heaven.

Heck, we'd be prouder'n a peacock with two tails.

Now don't that fry your tater?

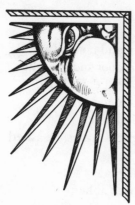

Front Porch Sayin's

When you set out to collect sayin's like these, you end up accumulatin' a whole slew of crazy, colorful stories to go along with 'em. One of my favorites is about Mrs. Sarah Ferguson, who lived in the small town in Kentucky where my friend Dave King spent his summers as a child. She lived on a hill in a big, white, three-story house next to the post office. It overlooked the parkin' lot for the drive-in movie theater that showed the raunchy late-night Saturday flicks Dave and his friends were forbidden to see. Mrs. Ferguson would sit and rock on her porch mendin' or stringin' beans or just watchin' the world go by, and nearly everyone in town would walk by and wave and say hello and make at least a little small talk on their way to pick up mail. Every once in awhile, Dave would stop too. Always, he was with his mom or dad or grandparents out runnin' errands or on their way to somewhere else. And, always, in amazement, he'd listen to the way Mrs. Ferguson would describe the weather. Never did he hear her use the same phrase twice.

One day, it'd be **"so dry, the fish are knockin' at my door and askin' for a drink of water."** The next time he saw her, she'd yell down **"hot enough to roast the devil, darlin'."**

Years later, when Mrs. Ferguson no longer spent her days outside and Dave was off at college, he returned to town for a weekend visit.

Alone this time, Dave stopped by the post office and noticed a frailer, thinner woman slip a hand out the screen door and grab the newspaper off the porch of the big white house next door. Dave called to her, hopin' she'd come back out and he'd get to hear another great ol' front porch phrase from his childhood.

He reminded her of who he was, then, after pleasantries, he asked about the weather.

"**Hotter than honeymooners' sheets,**" she said.

Dave looked down at his flannel shirt, then back at her.

She winked.

"Oh, you really mean the weather, don't you?" Mrs. Ferguson asked.

Dave nodded, as she pulled him closer and whispered in his ear. "Honey, it's not the weather I've been ratin' all those years. It's the movies."

Hot enough to fry pigeons on the wing.

Hot enough to fry spit.

Hot as a four-horned billy goat.

Hotter than a June bride.

So hot the hens are layin' hard-boiled eggs.

Hotter than a $2 pistol.

Hotter than Georgia asphalt.

❂

Hotter than a gnat on a pickup truck windshield.

❂

Hotter than a firecracker.

❂

Hotter than a hooker's doorknob on payday.

❂

Hotter'n a three-balled tomcat.

❂

Cold enough to freeze the ears off a brass monkey.

❂

Cold as a gravestone in January.

❂

Cold as a frog's behind.

❂

Cold as a banker's heart.

❂

Cold as a witch's tit in a brass bra.

Cold as a pickerel's prat.

Cold as an Alaskan well digger's belt buckle.

Colder than a mother-in-law's love.

Cold as a well rope.

Cold as a well-digger's ankle.

Colder than a well digger's destination.

Cold as a black freeze.

BRR-R-R

Cold as January.

So cold my tutu turned into a one-one.

It's comin' up a bad cloud.

Pourin' down bullfrogs.

❂

Rainin' pitchforks and babies.

❂

Rainin' like a cow peein' on a flat rock.

❂

It's a frog strangler.

❂

Rainin' so hard it'd make Noah's flood look like a mornin' dew.

❂

So wet my skin is sproutin' watercress.

❂

So wet we're shootin' ducks in the parlor.

❂

Wet as a widow's handkerchief.

So wet I've been catchin' catfish in the mousetraps.

●

Can't dance and it's too wet to plow.

●

Empty as a winter rain barrel.

●

So dry I could spit cotton.

●

River's so low we'll have to start haulin' water to it.

●

As sudden as a clap of thunder on a sunny day.

●

Disappeared like a belch in a wind storm.

●

The wind was so fierce it blew the varnish off the deck.

The wind was so fierce it blew the architecture off the house.

> ☯

The wind blew so hard a toothpick could drag a 100-pound anchor in a 50-foot well.

> ☯

The only sure thing about the weather is a dry spell always ends.

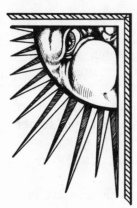

Kitchen Sayin's

Another of my favorite stories comes from a preacher from Tennessee named Everett Thomas, who spends a lot of time entertainin' other preachers passin' through from out of town. One of those, a heavy man named Angus Barrows, told him of his lifelong search for the world's best food. As soon as Rev. Thomas heard of his colleague's quest, he promised him he'd reach his goal in the mountains of Tennessee where home cookin' was an art form still practiced in local restaurants.

And so, after Sunday mornin' services, the two preachers headed to Rev. Thomas's favorite eatin' spot where Thomas proudly handed over a menu that listed all the specialties of the house — country ham with red-eye gravy, biscuits made with buttermilk, rich corn puddin', macaroni and cheese to die for and fried chicken that would make the colonel weep.

"I'm hungry enough to eat the handle off a hoe," Rev. Barrows told the hostess.

"Well, the food here is so good, it'd make a bulldog break its chain," she told him.

"Not good enough," Rev. Barrows bellowed and out the door he headed, Rev. Thomas at his heels.

The two drove on to Rev. Thomas's next favorite place where

Rev. Barrows scanned a second mouth-watering menu. **"I'm hungry enough to eat the butt off a rag doll,"** he told the hostess this time.

"Well," she said, **"the food here is so good that if you put it on top of your head, your tongue'd slap your brains out tryin' to get to it."**

"Not good enough," Rev. Barrows snorted and out the door he stormed.

Feelin' sheepish, Rev. Thomas drove him onto his next favorite spot.

"I'm hungry enough to eat the south end off a northbound skunk," Rev. Barrows told the hostess this time.

"Well, honey," she said, **"to get a better piece of chicken, you'd have to be a rooster."**

Rev. Barrows leaned up real close to her and smiled. "Cock-a-doodle-do," he said. "You got a table for two?"

Who blew your pilot light out?

ঔ

I'm hungry enough to eat a bull and beg for the horns.

ঔ

I'm hungry as a bug in a 'tater patch.

I'm so hungry I could lick the sweat off a cafeteria window.

◆

I'm hungry enough to eat the sideboards off a manure truck.

◆

I could eat a span of mules and chew hell outta the driver.

◆

My backbone's rubbin' my belly.

◆

I'll eat anything that doesn't eat me first.

◆

It disappeared like a T-bone steak in a dog pound.

◆

It's so good it'd make a freight train take a dirt road.

◆

It's better'n a cold collard sandwich.

◆

I ate so much I ran aground.

I'm as full as an egg.

🐦

My stomach's full but my mouth ain't satisfied.

🐦

Everything's chicken but the bill.

🐦

He ate that chicken 'til it was slick as a ribbon.

🐦

Eatin' the gospel bird. (That's chicken - served on Sunday.)

🐦

It's nothin' a little chicken soup won't fix.

🐦

He doesn't know chalk from cheese.

🐦

He's teachin' his grandmother to suck eggs.

🐦

Scarce as a deviled egg after
a church picnic.

Butter wouldn't melt in her mouth.

❂

Slower'n cream risin' on last year's buttermilk.

❂

Slower'n molasses tryin' to run uphill in January.

❂

She's heavier'n a ton o' lard in a molasses can.

❂

Beans ain't beans without sow belly.

❂

Don't that fry your tater?

❂

You can't warm over cold potatoes.

❂

Don't get your meat and potatoes in the same place.

❂

I've seen cows hurt worse than this get better. (What you say when your steak's too rare.)

❂

We ate everything on that hog 'cept the squeal.

Tender as a judge's heart.

Slick as a peeled onion.

Short as pie crust.

Easy as nailin' Jello to the wall.

Dried out as a prune.

Flaky as a bowl of a cereal.

Easy as lickin' dew off a rose bush.

You're sweeter'n saccharin at a drugstore sale.

She can cook a pancake so thin it's only got one side to it.

She could stick her finger in a cow pie and I'd eat it.

She could cook road kill and I'd eat it.

🜨

She couldn't boil water without scorchin' it.

🜨

She couldn't boil water or burn bread.

🜨

That coffee was so strong it could stand up by itself.

🜨

That coffee was so weak I had to help it out of the pot.

🜨

She never lets that pickle out of the jar. (She keeps a tight rein on him.)

🜨

She wouldn't work in a pie factory.

She's dish-throwin' mad.

❂

He's an appetite with skin drawn over it.

❂

He had the appetite of an Alaskan grizzly after hibernation.

❂

He's got the missed-meal colic.

❂

He got fried in his own grease.

❂

He's puttin' on his company manners.

❂

He talks like he's gotta mouth fulla mush.

❂

Call me anything but late for dinner.

❂

Don't quarrel with your bread and butter.

❂

I didn't just roll into town on a head of lettuce.

I feel like the underside of a turnip green. (Low and green.)

❧

I got through that like a slick bucket of boiled okra.

❧

I'm hangin' in there like a hair in a biscuit.

❧

I feel like the butter's slipped off my biscuit.

❧

That's a lot a stirrin' and no biscuits.

❧

I'd rather eat a bug.

❧

I'm old and ugly but I can still pull up to the table three times a day.

❧

I've got my mouth all poked out for . . . (I'm hungry for . . .)

❧

I like my fish lookin' at me. (I like my fish with the head on.)

Put the big pot in the little one. (Try to impress someone.)

Ə

The more you stir the pot the worse it stinks.

Ə

They're as different as oil and water.

You can't make pound cake outta cow manure.

Ə

You can't chew with somebody else's teeth.

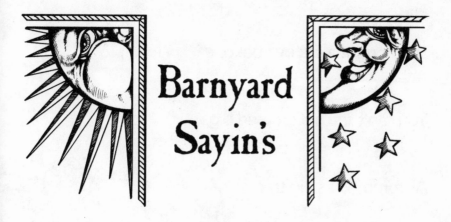

Barnyard Sayin's

And then there's the story of the city boy who's visiting his country cousins who take him to the Saturday night dance at the fire hall.

When one of the local girls asks him to dance, he says "no thanks."

"There's no mistakin' you for a hayseed," he tells her. **"You're tough as cowhide, out there struttin' like a chicken with a behind like a Tennessee walker."**

"You know," says the country girl, "I'm a little confused. Here you are, a guy from the big city and **you're rough as goat guts, out there steppin' like a rooster in deep mud and hung like a chicken."**

Here are a few more sayin's from the barnyard that'll shut nearly anyone up.

Happier than a pig in slop.

❧

Happier than a dead pig in the sunshine.

She bought a pig in a poke.

You can't catch a greased pig.

As common as pig tracks.

Slippery as pig salve.

Well tie me to an ol' fat sow and drag me through a trough o' slop.

He sings like a bellyachin' hog.

I haven't had this much fun since the hogs ate my little brother.

That fits like a hog in a saddle.

Useless as tits on a boar hog.

Nervous as a hen on a hot griddle.

Scarce as hen's teeth.

Hoverin' like a hen with one chick.

They jumped on it like a chicken on a worm.

That's like throwin' a fox into a chicken house.

You've got no more chance than a grasshopper in a chicken house.

Runnin' 'round like a chicken with its head cut off.

I could chase a chicken 'round the barn, I'm so tickled.

When the foxes pack the jury box, the chicken's always guilty.

That's like tryin' to sneak sunup past a rooster.

❂

I spoke to her and she didn't say pea turkey squat.

❂

He's prouder'n a peacock with two tails.

❂

Quicker'n crap through a goose.

❂

Blind as Dillard's mule.

❂

Noisier'n a mule in a tin barn.

❂

That's about as sexy as socks on a rooster.

❂

Mad as a mule chewin' on bumblebees.

❂

He's got enough money to burn a mule.

❂

Stout as a mule.

Don't worry about the mule goin' blind, just load the wagon.

❂

She could talk the ears off a mule.

❂

She's got more than one mule in her stable.

❂

Don't beat a dead horse.

❂

A fartin' horse never tires.

❂

Hold your horses.

❂

That's a horse of a different color.

❂

You shut the barn door after the horse got out.

❂

She could make a horse laugh.

❂

Don't look a gift horse in the mouth.

Travelin' by shank's mare.

Prouder'n a stallion out to stud.

Staggerin' 'round like a blind horse in a punkin patch.

Just milk the cow, don't pull the udder off.

Dark as the inside of a cow.

Money's like cow manure. It don't do no good until you spread it around.

Clumsy as a bull in a china shop.

Useful as a bucket under a bull.

🔊

I was as surprised as if a sheep had bit me.

🔊

You don't have the sense God gave a billy goat.

Over the Back Fence Sayin's

Some folks call it gossip. To us it's just bein' a good neighbor, fillin' folks in on how we're gettin' along or tellin' 'em exactly what we think about how somebody else is gettin' along.

These are the sayin's you hear just about everywhere, at the corner store, post office, on the telephone. But the best and longest uninterrupted string of 'em I ever heard was at a church bazaar where Vera Darnell, the town gossip, was sittin' around a table with a dozen other women sortin' and pricin' home-made jam and crocheted crafts. She just happened to mention that Dee Dee Gibson, that's *Mrs.* Bobby Gibson, and Bubba Riley got apprehended in the act the night before by *Mrs.* Bubba Riley.

"He sure got caught with his pants down," said Thelma Thompson.

"He was so surprised you coulda knocked his eyes off with a stick," said Mrs. Castle, sittin' next to her.

"He was nervous as a porcupine in a balloon factory," Mrs. Thurston said before the woman next to her spoke up.

"He's in more trouble than if he was holdin' a bear's tail," she said.

And so it went, around the table, with not a one of 'em even stoppin' for a second to think about what they might be sayin'.

"There he was, sowin' his wild oats and hopin' for crop failure."

"Yeah, he doesn't know the difference between come here and sic 'em."

"Well, I'm tellin' you, she's a time bomb with the pin pulled."

"She's always showin' more meat than a butcher shop window."

"Heck, she's been married so many times she has veil rash."

"Ain't that the cotton-pickin' truth."

"Well roll me up and call me curly."

Here's a list of what else you mighta heard if there'd been a few hundred more folks sittin' 'round that table. They'll tickle the tar outta ya.

He'd fight a circle saw.

🎵

He's got more holes in his head than a pin cushion.

🎵

He's so dumb he went loggin' and cut down the family tree.

🎵

He's got some buttons missin'.

🎵

She's got a bee in her bonnet.

🎵

He's a lost ball in high weeds.

He's only got 50 cards in his deck.

❂

He's soft in the head.

❂

He's a little weak in the intellectuals.

❂

He's yodelin' in a canyon.

❂

He's all vines and no taters.

❂

He's an empty sack.

❂

Her lid's not on too tight.

❂

She ain't all there.

❂

Of all the things I've lost I miss my mind the most.

❂

He's got a mind like flypaper.

He's as mixed up as a fart in a hurricane.

I'm as busy as a bee in a tar bucket.

I'm as busy as a one-armed paperhanger.

I'm so busy I don't have
time to cuss the cat.

I'm so busy I met myself
in the hallway.

I'm as busy as a barefoot boy in an ant bed.

I'm busier than a man with one hole and two snakes.

I'm busier than a one-armed fiddler with the crabs.

He moves like the lice is fallin' off a him.

He was movin' so slow dead flies wouldn't fall
off a him.

He's so slow it takes him an hour and a half to watch
"60 Minutes."

He's all behind like a fat woman. (He's late.)

As lazy as Uncle Deal.

He's so lazy he's got calluses on his butt.

He's so lazy he stops plowin' to fart.

He's self-employed and he still got fired.

He'll never drown in sweat.

He hasn't hit a lick at a snake. (He hasn't worked in
awhile.)

He hung around like dead lice.

The hurrier I go the behinder I get.

It's as easy as shootin' flies off a watermelon.

It's as easy as swallowin' a mosquito.

It's as easy as rollin' off a log.

It's like tryin' to lasso the invisible man.

It's like tryin' to poke a cat out from under the porch with a rope.

Useful as a screen door on a submarine.

Trapped like a fart in a pair of panty hose.

❂

I don't know her from Adam's house cat.

❂

He doesn't have a leg to stand on.

❂

He's got his feet firmly planted in quicksand.

❂

His feet were so big, he had to go down to the crossroads to turn around.

❂

His feet were so big, he had to put his britches on over his head.

❂

He has two left feet.

❂

He can smell a small mouse quicker'n a starvin' cat.

❂

If the shoe fits it won't hurt your foot.

It's as comfortable as an old shoe.

His feet were so tough, he wore his shoes out from the inside.

My home town was so tough, we ate barbed wire and thought it was candy.

Tougher'n woodpecker lips.

Tough as briars.

I can't stand it any more and I don't even know what it is.

I feel like a banjo; everybody's pickin' on me.

I felt like a bastard at a family reunion.

It's so sad it'd bring a tear to a glass eye.

All my friends are named Bill.

❂

I feel lower'n a snake in snowshoes.

I feel lower'n spots on a snake's tail.

❂

Happy as a clam at high tide.

❂

I wouldn't have her if she was strung with gold.

❂

I didn't take her to raise.

❂

He's growin' like a bad weed.

❂

Older'n dirt.

❂

He was old when New Orleans was a blueprint.

Snow on the roof doesn't mean there's no fire in the furnace.

The older the fiddle, the better the tune.

She's got more wrinkles than a washboard.

In a hundred years we'll all be bald.

I'm not bald. That's the solar panel for a sex machine.

I've seen better hair on a piece of meat.

I've seen better hair on a coconut.

I haven't seen hide nor hair of him.

You can't trust him any farther than you can see up an alligator's ass at midnight.

He's as crazy as a road lizard.

He got that at a five-fingered discount.

If you shake his hand, count your fingers.

He got that at a five-fingered discount.

He sold me down the river.

He could sell an anchor to a drownin' man.

He's armed for bear.

He's as crazy as a three-legged grasshopper.

Crazier'n a loon.

I'd rather watch grass grow.

❂

Excitin' as watchin' clothes dry.

❂

It went over like a pregnant pole vaulter.

❂

He'd skin a flea for its hide.

❂

He'd steal a chaw of tobacco out of your mouth.

❂

He'll pinch a nickel 'til the buffalo bleeds dry.

❂

He's so tight, he squeaks when he walks.

❂

She was cryin' and slingin' snot.

❂

She was havin' a conniption fit.

❂

She was pitchin' a hissy fit.

He flung a Joe Blizzard fit.

❂

He's got the fidgets worse'n a lizard.

❂

She's a caution.

❂

He's lookin' every which way but right.

❂

He's two jumps ahead of a fit.

❂

He's a dancin' fool.

❂

If she heard that, she'd lay square eggs.

❂

She doesn't know whether she's comin' or goin'.

❂

She's got her panties in a wad.

❂

We were tearin' up Jack.

Does a cat have claws?

🌑

Does a fat girl fart?

🌑

Is a pig's butt pork?

🌑

Are there cows in Texas?

🌑

We were so poor, mama had to cut holes in our pockets so we had something to play with.

🌑

Don't that beat all?

🌑

Don't that cock your pistol?

🌑

Don't that frost your punkin?

🌑

Who gives a tick?

🌑

I snored so loud, I had to sleep across the street from myself.

I've got so many holes in my mattress, it might as well be spring.

🖙

I'm too poor to pay attention.

🖙

We were so poor, we lived on grits and grunts.

🖙

If fat geese were sellin' for 10 cents a pound, I couldn't buy a hummingbird.

🖙

We were so poor, we didn't have a pot to pee in or a window to throw it out of.

🖙

I'm as broke as a con.

🖙

I'm so broke, I couldn't spend the night.

🖙

I'm so broke, I can't afford yesterday's newspaper.

🖙

If it cost a dollar to go around the world, I couldn't get out of sight.

She ain't got two nickels to rub together.

❂

Money thinks I'm dead.

❂

He's got more money than he can jump over.

❂

He's got more money than a porcupine has quills.

❂

If I had his nose full of nickels, I'd never have to work again.

❂

If I had your money and you had a feather in your pants, we'd both be tickled to death.

❂

He's ridin' the gravy train.

❂

I knowed him when he didn't have enough influence to flag down a gut wagon.

❂

He thinks he's the biggest frog in the puddle.

He's got a face only his mother and God could love.

🌑

Beauty is only skin deep, but ugly's to the bone.

🌑

He looked like he had been beat through hell with a soot bag.

🌑

He looks like he's been drug through a knothole backwards.

🌑

He can fix anything from a broken heart to the crack of dawn.

🌑

Handy as a fart in a phone booth.

🌑

Handier than a pocket on a shirt.

🌑

Ill as a hornet.

🌑

Ill as an ol' sore-tailed cat.

Iller'n a channel crab.

Don't blow a gasket.

Don't knock it until you've tried it.

Don't pee on my back and tell me it's rainin'.

Don't get your bowels in an uproar.

He'd climb a tree to tell a lie when he could stay on the ground and tell the truth.

He's a little economical with the truth.

One of 'em'll lie and the other one'll swear to it.

Limber as a dishrag.

Grimy as a mudflap at a tractor-pull.

Mad as fire.

❃

His steam is high enough to burst his boilers.

❃

Shakin' like a pair of dice.

❃

Noisy as a jarfly.

❃

Mad enough to bite a nail in two.

❃

Noisier'n skeletons makin' love on a tin roof.

❃

He was shakin' so bad, he couldn't take a dump in a 10-acre field.

❃

False as a mother-in-law's love.

❃

Fair as your hand.

❃

Straight as a hoe handle.

Little as a skeeter bump.

Wild as a buck.

Rough as a cob.

Hard as a boiled cannon.

Hard as a lightard knot.

Hard as Chinese arithmetic.

So hard the cat couldn't scratch it.

Dark as two black cats in a coal pile at night.

Fast as all get out.

Fine as frog hair.

Fine as frog hair split up the middle and tied at both ends.

Flat as a flitter.

Flat as a fritter.

Gooder'n snuff.

Green as a gourd.

Bigger'n a thunder squall and twice as mean.

Mean as snake venom.

He can eat sawdust and crap 2 X 4s.

He can swallow iron and crap bullets.

He really crapped in his mess kit.

Quick as a coiled snake.

❂

Quick as a chipmunk.

❂

Quicker'n a cat
can lick its butt.

❂

Quiet as a mouse peein' into a cotton ball.

❂

Red as the taillights on a tin lizzy.

❂

Deaf as a post.

❂

Tough as a pine knot.

❂

Wilder'n a panther cat.

❂

Slicker'n a greased eel.

❂

Tight as Dick's hatband.

Tight as chicks in a nest.

Tight as the bark on a hickory log.

Tighter'n a duck's ass.

Tighter'n the pin feathers on a prairie chicken's butt.

Tighter'n a tick's ass over a rain barrel.

You're so tight, you'd need a sledgehammer to drive a flax seed up your butt.

Shiny as a pistol.

Slippery as a wet log.

Slower'n bread mold.

Sour as a pelican's breath.

Smooth as silk.

Delicate as cobwebs.

Determined as rain.

Faster than greased lightnin'.

Flashy as a rat with a gold tooth.

Sorry as owl shit.

As little in the waist as a sickly mud dauber.

Sore as four boils.

Sweatin' worse than a monkey tryin' to write a letter.

Scruffy lookin' as the hind wheels of hard luck.

His luck's so bad, his yo-yo won't even come back to him.

❂

Nervous as the end
of a rabbit's nose.

❂

Nervous as a
long-tailed cat
in a room full of rockin' chairs.

❂

He's so tall, he's got to climb a ladder to shave himself.

❂

She's so tall, she could stand flat-footed and pee into the radiator of a Chevy pickup.

❂

He's tall enough to go duck huntin' with a rake.

❂

She's just skin and bones.

❂

He was so skinny, a rattlesnake struck him five times in the leg and then went elsewhere.

He's so skinny, you have to shake the sheets to find him.

♻

He's no bigger than a minute.

♻

He's blind in one eye and can't see outta the other.

♻

He's blind as a deer in headlights.

♻

I don't know whether to shit or go blind. I think I'll just close one eye and fart.

♻

He's the red-headed step child.

♻

He's got more kin than a rabbit.

♻

There's a fly in the ointment.

♻

He's borin' with a mighty bit auger.

♻

He's courtin' disaster.

His butt's in a sling.

He's been puttin' out a fire with gunpowder.

You scared the daylights outta me.

You scared the pot liquor outta me.

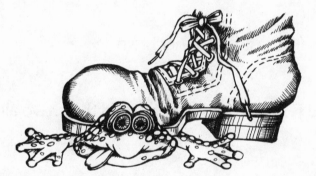

His eyes bugged out like a tromped-on toad-frog.

It's no bigger than the little end of nothin' whittled down to a fine point.

It's not worth a bucket of warm spit.

You're not worth a tinker's damn.

You're not worth a pewter button.

🕭

You're not worth the bullet it'd take to shoot you.

🕭

You're a pimple on the tail of progress.

🕭

He walks like a monkey on a string.

🕭

Her tongue flips faster than her brain.

🕭

I hardly said two words to her but I said them two all the time.

🕭

She's got foot-in-mouth disease.

🕭

He's talkin' under my clothes.

🕭

He sure put his foot in it.

Tryin' to convince her is like arguin' with a stump on fire.

❂

She could make people happy just by lettin' 'em alone.

❂

She deals in dirt.

❂

His voice is too loud for indoor use.

❂

Hip deep in alligators.

❂

He sure dropped his buckets.

❂

She's been around the block a time or two.

❂

She's had more pricks than a second-hand dart board.

❂

She gets around so much she keeps runnin' into herself.

She's been rode hard and put up wet.

If she had as many stickin' outta her as she had stuck in her she could wrestle a porcupine.

She runs around with riffraff.

She's no better than she should be.

She put a spoke in his wheel.

She's built like a brick outhouse.

That dress was about to eat her up.

She didn't have on enough clothes to pad a crutch.

He's all wool and a yard wide.

She makes all her own clothes.

❂

He's all belt and buckle.

❂

She'd cut the heart out of a good friend for a dollar.

❂

She's got a heart as big as her behind.

❂

She's always in somebody's crack.

❂

She's eat up with . . . (cancer, jealousy, etc.).

❂

She's a good shoulder baby.

❂

Hip to haunch and cheek to jowl.

❂

This place is so crowded, you'd have to go outside to change your mind.

❂

They cut a shine. (They were misbehavin'.)

They played the blixum. (They messed up.)

❂

They're makin' the beast with two backs.

❂

They tied the knot.

I need that about as much as a tomcat needs a marriage license.

❂

Bigamy is havin' one wife too many. Monogamy is the same.

❂

All marriages are happy, it's the livin' together afterward that causes all the trouble.

❂

He's exercisin' his marital rights.

❂

They split the quilt.

Ain't no never mind.

🕭

Angle Olly. (Turn left.)

🕭

I ain't seen you in a month of Sundays.

🕭

I've been ponderin' so hard, I ain't had time to think.

🕭

I can think but not today.

🕭

I need that like I need another hole in my head.

🕭

I didn't just fall off a turnip truck.

🕭

I just want the rubber band to stretch in all directions.

🕭

That's enough to gag a maggot.

🕭

That just sticks in my gizzard.

We didn't cotton to him.

❂

We've howdied, but we've not shook.

❂

You can't stop me from thinkin'.

❂

I suwannee. (I swear.)

❂

I'll be swiggered.

❂

For cryin' out loud.

❂

Gee Willikers.

❂

My hind foot.

❂

My stars and garters.

❂

That's more bubble gum than I can chew.

That gripes my middle kidney.

🕭

You took the words right out of my mouth.

🕭

You're a sight for sore eyes.

🕭

Well I'll be a monkey's uncle.

🕭

Well I'll be John Brown.

🕭

Well lay me down and turn me over.

🕭

That's a fine howdy do.

🕭

That's a hell of a way to run a railroad.

🕭

Every alley has its own tin can.

🕭

That's like stoppin' a clock to save time.

It's better'n snuff and half as dusty.

🔹

It's the best thing since the flush toilet.

🔹

It does my heart good.

🔹

It don't make no never mind to me.

🔹

It's sap-risin' time.

🔹

I laughed so hard, I popped my gizzard string.

🔹

It'd take a Philadelphia lawyer to figure that out.

🔹

Make hay while the sun shines.

🔹

A little bit of powder and a little bit of paint makes a woman look like what she ain't.

🔹

What God's forgotten, you can stuff with cotton.

🔹

A narrow mind has a broad tongue.

A new broom sweeps clean.

❂

There's no accountin' for taste.

The apple doesn't fall far from the tree.

❂

The bigger a man's head is, the easier it is to fill his shoes.

❂

The difference between adults and children is adults don't ask questions.

❂

If it ain't one thing, it's another.

❂

You know you've reached middle age when all you exercise is caution.

❂

Take your problems as they come if you think you can handle them that fast.

❂

Advice is worth what you pay for it.

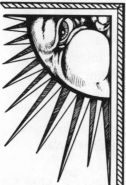

Woodshed Sayin's

Woodshed sayin's are the ones your father used when he was really mad. Things like, "if you don't quit that, **I'm gonna cloud up and rain all over you.**" My favorite story about them comes from my uncle, who grew up in the coal-mined hills of southern Ohio after the Great Depression. In the years between his boyhood and his teens, he hung out with a gangly group of kids with names like Buster, Buck, Red and Hobbs. They spent their days killin' time, avoidin' chores and lookin' for adventure. And Elphus Dowdy was always gettin' in their way.

They knew him as "the bachelor," the mean ol' man whose yard had the shortcut to the woods runnin' through it. Ol' man Dowdy hated those kids and that shortcut as much as he loved to load buckshot. The bachelor'd spend his days waitin' for the boys to head home from school so he could set about the task of tryin' to sting a half dozen pair of skinny, agile, adolescent legs. The whole time he'd be yellin' things like "When I get my hands on you, **I'm gonna slap the daylights outta every one of you.**" When that got no reaction, he'd get rougher. "When I get ahold a you," he'd yell in a voice as wobbly as his ol' legs, **"I'm gonna stomp a mudhole in you then stomp it dry."**

The boys would laugh, makin' ol' man Dowdy even madder.

He'd yell louder and shoot faster, and the kids would taunt him more and so the cycle went. Then, one day, the skinniest boy of all, the one they all called Pencil, took a dare, walked right up on the bachelor's porch and knocked. When ol' man Dowdy answered, he let lose with the worst insult he could think of. **"If I had a dog with a face as ugly as yours,"** Pencil said, as he watched ol' man Dowdy reachin' for his gun, **"I'd shave his butt and teach him to walk backwards."**

But ol' man Dowdy, with just the slightest grin spreadin' 'cross his face, had a comeback. **"I'm gonna slap you so hard, you're goin' to have to roll your socks down so you can use the outhouse,"** he hissed at Pencil. And he never bothered those boys again.

I'm gonna jerk you through a knot.

❷

I'm gonna knock the ugly outta you.

❷

I'm gonna smack you so hard, you're going to hum like a 10-penny finishing nail hit with a greasy ball peen hammer.

❷

I'm gonna slap you so hard, when you quit rollin' your clothes'll be outta style.

❷

I'll slap the snot outta you.

❷

I'll knock you into next week.

I'm gonna slap you so hard, your teeth'll come out single file.

I'll be on you like a duck on a June bug.

I'll get all over you like white on rice.

I'll stick to you like ugly
on an ape.

I'll give you a dose of your own medicine.

I'll give you a dose that'll puken you worsen lobelia.

I'm gonna put a five-gallon can of whup-ass on you.

I'm gonna wipe the floor up with you.

I'm gonna wear you out.

I'm gonna hit you so hard, your kids'll be born dumb.

That ought to cork your pistol.

❧

You're askin' for a pine box.

Fishin' Hole Sayin's

Everybody knows **how far a fisherman stretches the truth depends on the length of his arms** and that **nothin' grows faster than a fish from the time it bites 'til it gets away.**

But we've got a fishin' story we know is true, 'cuz it comes from our brother, Mike.

He was out with his buddies fishin' one day tellin' 'em about another time he was out on the lake when this skunk tied with twine to an encyclopedia came floatin' by. A couple of the other guys leaned over the boat and tried to net the skunk 'cuz they knew nobody was gonna believe this story. But every time they got close, the skunk sprayed 'em.

When they finally got home that night, their wives wanted to know why they smelled so much worse than usual. No matter how hard they tried, they couldn't get the women to believe their story.

"I don't know why they didn't buy it," Mike told the guys on this trip. "The smell shoulda been proof enough."

"Well, did your wife believe it?" asked another guy.

"Heck, yeah," said Mike, "she bought it book, twine and stinker."

We'd tell you some of his other fishin' stories, but all the good ones got away. So these sayin's'll hafta do.

To catch a big fish, you need a stiff pole.

❂

Fish or cut bait.

❂

He drinks like a fish.

❂

Fishin' without beer makes the day last a year.

❂

She swallowed it hook, line and sinker.

❂

Easy as shootin' fish in a barrel.

❂

Squirmin' like a worm in hot ashes.

❂

Quick as a minnow.

❂

He's as crooked as a black snake.

❂

The mosquitoes around here are so big, they could stand flat footed and bugger a tom turkey.

He hung on like a snapper on a fisherman's toe.

❂

If you threw him in the river, he'd come up with a fish.

❂

She's in cooter heaven.

❂

He's as disorganized as a bucket of worms.

❂

She's a keeper.

❂

Water's so low, the fish are gettin' freckle-faced.

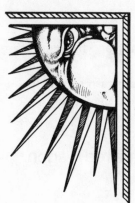

Hayloft
Sayin's

The beauty of so many of these sayin's lies in the personal memories they bring back to us when we remember the first time we heard them or a favorite relative who used them.

Take our friend Jacki Winters.

She grew up in Kentucky, about 60 miles east of Lexington, and from the time she was 7, she'd spend her weekends out in the country with her grandparents. Pappaw worked the coal mines and at the brickyard and farmed tobacco on the side. Jacki remembers ridin' in the pickup between him and Mammaw, complainin' about his slow drivin'. Sometimes, she'd mash her little foot on top of his to get him to speed up. And sometimes the three of them would go for walks or pick up a bucket of chicken and have a picnic or Jacki would climb trees and Pappaw would tease her from down below. **"Just think of how tall you'd be if half your legs hadn't grown into feet,"** he'd yell up to her.

And then, every Sunday, when little Jacki was gettin' ready to leave, she'd turn to Pappaw, give him a big hug and say "I love you."

"Me too," he'd say. He just couldn't bring himself to say those three words back.

Twenty years later, after Mammaw died, Jacki was back visitin' him again. "I love you," she told him as she left.

"I love you more than the cat loves the cream jar," he told her back.

Pappaw knew that sometimes "I love you" just wasn't enough. For those occasions, we offer up these sayin's from the hayloft.

You're pretty as a speckled pup under a red wagon.

❂

You're pretty as a spotted horse in a daisy pasture.

❂

My heart's flutterin' like a duck in a puddle.

❂

You're the duck's quack.

❂

You're the tiger's spots.

❂

You're cute as a bug's ear.

❂

You're as hot as a billy goat in a pepper patch.

❂

Sure as the vine twines 'round the stump, you are my darlin' sugar lump.

Love may not make the world go 'round, but it sure makes the ride worthwhile.

Ͽ

I wouldn't trade you for a farm in Georgia.

Ͽ

As long as I gotta biscuit, you got half.

Ͽ

Let's swap slobbers.

Ͽ

Lay down, I think I love you.

School Yard Sayin's

And then there's our ol' schoolteacher friend Susan Huntley who's always tellin' us how much you can learn from kids these days.

To prove her point, she invited us to spend a day with her 23 fourth-graders at Thomas Edison Elementary School in York, S.C.

Everything seemed just like we remembered it way back when until recess when a fight broke out and children started screamin' insults at each other like we had never heard.

"We just don't understand kids today," we told Susan.

"All you need to do is listen and you can figure 'em out," she told us.

Just then, one little boy yelled to a girl, **"You're so ugly, the tide won't take you out."**

We looked at Susan.

"He grew up on the coast," she told us.

Then the girl yelled back, ""Oh, yeah," she said, **"You're so dumb you couldn't find the sofa in your own living room."**

"Her mother is a sales clerk at the furniture store," Susan told us.

Then another boy jumped in. **"The truth ain't in you, your feet stink and you don't love Jesus,"** he yelled.

"Baptist," Susan said.

Read on. We bet we've got a few that are just right for you too.

You're dumber than a box of rocks.

🌑

You're so dumb, if you fell into a barrel full of tits you'd come out suckin' your thumb.

🌑

You're a pickle shy of a Whopper.

🌑

You're three sandwiches short of a picnic.

🌑

You're two shrimp short of a cocktail.

🌑

You're three bricks shy of a load.

🌑

You're a few green stamps short of a toaster.

🌑

You're dumb as a dishrag.

🌑

You're dumb as dirt.

🌑

You're so dumb, if they put your brain on the head of a pin it would roll around like a BB on a six-lane highway.

You're livin' in a 100-watt world with a 40-watt mind.

You can't count to 10 without takin' your shoes off.

You'd scratch your butt if your head itched.

You're so dumb, you'd go after a chicken's butt for a hot egg sandwich.

You couldn't pull a greased string out of a porcupine's butt.

You couldn't find your butt with both hands and a map.

You can't tell owl crap from putty without a map.

You ain't got the sense God gave lettuce.

You don't have enough sense to pour piss out of a boot.

You'd screw up a three-bean dinner.

You don't know beans when the bag's open.

You don't know nits from noodles.

You couldn't find water at the ocean.

You're duller than the blade on a widow's axe.

You couldn't hit a bull in the butt with a bass fiddle.

You can't walk and chew gum at the same time.

🜚

An idea would bust your head wide open.

🜚

You ain't got all your buttons.

🜚

You couldn't get elected dogcatcher.

🜚

You couldn't hit water if you fell off a boat.

🜚

You couldn't organize beer in a brewery.

You don't have sense enough to pound sand into a rat hole.

🜚

You're about a half bubble off plumb.

🜚

You're not too tightly wrapped.

You're not wearin' a full string of beads.

❂

You've got a few lights out on your marquee.

❂

You've got bats in your belfry.

❂

You've got bees in your bonnet.

❂

You've got toys in your attic.

❂

You've only got one oar in the water.

❂

Your cheese has slipped off your cracker.

❂

Your elevator doesn't go all the way to the top.

❂

Your telephone's ringin' but nobody's answerin'.

❂

Your roof ain't nailed on tight.

You were behind the door when brains were passed out.

🕭

If you had bird brains, you'd fly backwards.

🕭

You're as ugly as a mud fence daubed with tadpoles.

🕭

You're as ugly as homemade lye soap.

🕭

You're so ugly, a fly wouldn't light on you.

🕭

You're so ugly, they had to tie a pork chop around your neck to get the dog to play with you.

🕭

You're so ugly, you could scare a bulldog off a meat truck.

🕭

You're so ugly, you could snag lightnin'.

🕭

You're so ugly, you have to sneak up on a glass of water to get a drink.

You're so ugly, you have to whip your feet to get 'em into bed with you at night.

You're so ugly, your mother had to borrow a baby to take to church.

If you had my butt, you'd be two-faced.

You look like you got beat with an ugly stick.

You look like somebody tried to beat out a fire on your face with the flat side of a shovel.

You might be ugly, but you're stupid too.

Your face is as ugly as a stack of black cats with their tails cut off.

Your face is so ugly, you wore out two bodies.

You're ugly enough to stop an eight-day clock.

Your face might not stop a clock, but it'd sure raise hell with small watches.

You were born ugly and backslid.

You look like you fell out of the ugly tree and hit every limb on the way down.

You're so ugly, when you were born the doctor slapped your momma.

You're so ugly, your momma won't let you in the woods for fear you'll scare the bears.

You're so ugly, your momma sets you in a corner and feeds you with a slingshot.

You're so ugly, you have to slap yourself to sleep.

You're ugly enough to curdle milk.

You look like you got in a hatchet fight and lost your hatchet.

I've seen better faces on an iodine bottle.

You look like you could suck the chrome off a trailer hitch.

What would you charge to haunt a house?

You can't help bein' ugly, but you could stay home.

You're as ugly as a barrel full of beer farts.

You're as big as a skinned mule and twice as ugly.

You're so fat, if you had to haul ass it'd take two trips.

You've got more chins than a Chinese phone book.

You're so fat, it'd take two men and a boy just to look at you.

You're as crazy as a monkey in itchin' powder.

You're as crazy as a one-legged toad frog.

You're as crazy as a peach-orchard boar.

You're as crazy as a bullbat.

You're so lazy, you wouldn't holler sooey if the hogs was eatin' you.

Your breath smells like you chewed your socks.

You're so bowlegged, you couldn't hem a hog in a ditch.

❸

You're so bowlegged, you couldn't hem a shoat up in a corner.

❸

You're so bucktoothed, you could eat an apple through a picket fence.

❸

You're so cross-eyed, you can look at your own head.

❸

You're so cross-eyed, you got one eye lookin' at a snake and the other lookin' for somethin' to kill it with.

❸

You're so cross-eyed, when you cry tears run down your back.

❸

You couldn't carry a tune in a bucket.

❸

You couldn't bust a light bulb with a ball peen hammer.

You don't have no more chance than a one-legged man in an ass-kickin'.

❀

You're so short I'd have to dig a hole to kick your butt.

❀

You've got the personality of a dishrag.

❀

You don't have a snowball's chance in hell.

❀

You're as crooked as a barrel of fish hooks.

❀

You're not worth the powder and shot it'd take to blow you to kingdom come.

❀

You're so low-down, you could crawl under a snake's belly.

❀

You're so stingy, you wouldn't pay a nickel to see a pissant eat a bale of hay.

❀

I hear you're close related to the smallpox on your mother's side.

I wouldn't piss on you if you were on fire.

Your pickup couldn't pull a fat baby off a tricycle.

You abbreviated piece
a nothin'.

You toilet fish.

I wouldn't give you air if you were in a jug.

I wouldn't touch you with a barge pole.

I'd kick your balls through your brains if you had
either.

You couldn't get lucky if you were in a women's
prison with a handful of paroles.

You're a half-baked yokum.

You lie like a rug.

You lie like a rug.

Go take a powder.

Go butt a stump.

Sunday-go-to-Meetin' Sayin's

Preachers, as you know, have some of the best stories and sayin's. This is another one from our Tennessee friend Rev. Thomas, who was just relaxin' at home one night when a feverish knock at the door interrupted him. When he opened it, there stood Jimmy Hill shakin' and a sputterin' so bad, the preacher could hardly understand him. When the reverend finally got him calmed down, Jimmy told him he wanted to be married right there that night to his sweetheart, Thelma, who he just found out was in a family way.

"Her daddy says if I'm not married to her by the end of the day, I'll be buried by the end of the week," Jimmy told him.

Rev. Thomas married Jimmy and Thelma that night and they had their little girl and everything worked out just fine. Years later, the preacher saw the couple in church with all three of their younguns and reminded them of that night.

"Yeah," said Jimmy. **"I was as nervous as a hooker in church."**

"I've seen hookers in church," the preacher told him. "You weren't that nervous."

"I wasn't?" Jimmy asked, surprised.

"Nope," said Rev. Thomas, "You were **as nervous as a Christian Scientist with appendicitis."**

Virtue is its own punishment.

Well, bless your heart.

He's poorer'n a church mouse.

He's richer'n God.

From now until Gabriel blows his trumpet.

He's wearin' his Sunday-go-to-meetin' clothes.

I love you better'n Peter loved the Lord.

You wouldn't be happy sittin' on a log beside the Lord.

It's like I died and went to heaven.

Truer'n the book of Genesis.

Poor as Job's turkey.

❧

Quiet as sinners
on Sunday.

❧

He's got more problems than he can say grace over.

❧

Hotter'n the hinges of hell.

❧

Thicker'n fiddlers in hell.

❧

This world's goin' to hell in a hand basket.

He'd charge hell with a bucket of water to see if he
could put the fire out.

Even the devil will swear on a stack of Bibles.

He ran like the devil was after him.

I hate that the way Satan hates holy water.

It looks like Satan had a fit in here.

Heaven doesn't want me and the devil won't take me.

She's a street angel and a home devil.

He's too lazy to commit a sin.

Now tell that to the preacher.

Sayin's to Get Liquored Up By

Our friend Lolo, who used to be a bartender, had hundreds of great tavern stories for us. Only trouble is, she couldn't remember a one of 'em.

As she says, it doesn't matter where you are — sittin' around the still, bellyin' up to the country club bar or sneakin' a snort from your hip flask — all that matters is that you're drinkin' liquor. Unless, of course, you're **havin' a nip, downin' a shot, soakin' up the sauce, wallowin' in firewater, gettin' hammered, oiled, sloshed or juiced on rot gut, holy water or coffin varnish.**

Name your poison. Whatever you choose, Lolo says these saloon sayin's are bound to come in handy.

I'm dryer'n a powder house.

I'm so dry, I couldn't get wet in a shower.

Liquor up front, poker in the rear.

This'll put hair on your chest.

This'll put lead in your pencil.

It's good for what ails you and if nothin' ails you it's good for that too.

That whiskey's as smooth as the inside of a schoolteacher's thigh.

You need the hair of the dog that bit ya.

He tied one on.

He's feelin' no pain.

He's three sheets to the wind.

❂

He's as high as a Georgia pine.

❂

He was so drunk, he couldn't see through a ladder.

He was drunk as a boiled owl.

❂

He's so drunk, he looks like he's been bit by the brewer's dog.

❂

He was so drunk, he opened his shirt collar to take a leak.

He drinks liquor like he's suckin' buttermilk through a punkin stem.

He's close to knee walkin'.

❂

It don't take backbone to belly up to a bar.

❂

Liquor'll preserve anything but a secret.

❂

You ought not get loaded at the same time your gun is.

❂

I can resist anything but temptation.

❂

He copped the fifth quicker'n a drunk in a liquor store.

❂

I'd rather give up eatin'.

❂

That stuff'll make you slap your grandmother.

She was a moonshiner's daughter, but I loved her still.

Doggone Sayin's

Until now, each chapter has focused on a different country spot — the barn, outhouse, corner bar. But there are a few things besides places that are important enough to demand their own category when it comes to country sayin's: gifts of life so highly esteemed they generate their own body of wit and wisdom. Things that are as precious as life itself. Most important of those, of course, is man's best friend.

No other animal has as many sayin's dedicated to it and none other is held in such high regard. You already know what we say about hogs, cows, chickens, mules and goats, and it ain't pretty.

We were gonna tell you a great dog story from our friend Doug, but he lies so much he has to get his neighbor to call his dog. So just go ahead and read through these. Every one of em' is guaranteed to make you as happy as a wet dog next to a warm stove.

Barefooted as a yard dog.

Happier'n a dog waggin' two tails.

Happier'n a dog in a meat-packin' house.

Happy as a tick in a lap dog's crotch.

Shakin' like a wet dog in a cold wind.

Shakin' like a dog passin' a peach seed.

Shakin' like a dog passin' a log chain and dreadin' the hook.

Runnin' like a scalded dog.

Sneaky as a sheep-killin' dog.

Subtle as a dog with a woody.

He could talk a dog down off a meat wagon.

I ain't got no dog in that fight.

I ain't your porch dog.

❂

I'm goin' to see a man about a dog.

❂

It's so hot, if a dog went runnin' its shadow would drop down to rest.

❂

You look like the dogs had you under the house.

❂

Thick as the fleas on a dog's back.

❂

Puttin' on the dog.

❂

His bark is worse than his bite.

❂

You're barkin' up the wrong tree.

❂

A barkin' dog never bites.

❂

She thinks she's pertier'n a yellow dog with red eyeballs.

That dog won't hunt.

He went off with his tail between his legs.

He's runnin' with the hare and huntin' with the hounds.

Let's not drag that dog across the road anymore.

The sun don't set on one dog's butt all the time

I'm stayin' in this race 'til the last dog dies.

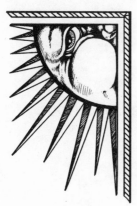

Mama's Sayin's

Of course mama deserves her own category too. It's hard to forget all the sayin's she used to keep us in line and comfort us. Her sayin's fell into two categories. First were the ones she used when things weren't goin' your way. Sayin's like **"He's not the only pebble on the beach"** or **"There are plenty of rolls in the bakery."** The others were the ones she used when things weren't goin' her way. You probably remember those better. Sayin's like **"What in the Sam Hill are you doin'?"** or **"You'll do what I say if you know what's good for you."**

It's that second category that gets passed from generation to generation more often than any other type of sayin'. Just ask your children.

And like momma would say, every darn one of 'em is **better'n a sharp stick in the eye. Now put that stick down before you poke somebody's eye out. If I've told you that once, I've told you 100 times . . . get back in here this minute young man . . .**

You're goin' up fool's hill on the slippery side.

It's a lot easier to dam a creek than a river.

❂

Stoppin' at third base is just as good as strikin' out.

❂

Don't rise above your raisin'.

❂

Don't split your britches.

❂

Don't be lollygaggin'.

❂

Quit that horseplay.

❂

Don't you sass me.

❂

Hush your mouth.

❂

Stop your bellyachin'.

❂

I'm gonna snatch the taste right outta your mouth.

❂

I'm gonna snatch you bald-headed.

Hold your tater.

🌀

You've got a mouth fulla gimmies.

You look like something the cat dragged in and the dog wouldn't eat.

🌀

You look like the tail end of hard times.

🌀

You look like you've been chewin' tobacco and spittin' into the wind.

🌀

You look like you washed in a mud puddle and combed your hair with a towel.

You look like you been sackin' bobcats and run outta sacks.

Actions speak louder than words.

An argument is just a swappin' of ignorance.

An empty barrel makes the most noise.

It sure is hard for an empty bag to stand up by itself.

Folks that get all wrapped up in themselves sure do make small packages.

Hard work never hurt anybody.

Ideas ain't gonna work unless you do.

You gotta paddle your own canoe.

🜨

You learn more listenin' than you do talkin'.

🜨

I ain't never had indigestion from swallowin' my pride.

🜨

If you can't say anything nice, don't say anything at all.

🜨

You don't have to
hang from a tree
to be a nut.

🜨

If you're goin' lookin' for trouble, you don't need to get ready for a long trip.

🜨

It's always best to stop and taste your words before you let 'em pass through your teeth.

🜨

I wouldn't hold in my hand what just came out of your mouth.

It's the last key that turns the lock.

Nothin' is beautiful from every point of view.

You can't get away from your raisin'.

There's a lid for every kettle.

There's a Jack for every Jill.

If you don't have somethin' for sale, don't advertise it.

Who licked the red off your candy?

What in tarnation are you doin'?

You ain't foolin' me none.

You made your bed, now lie in it.

A cow couldn't find her own calf in here.

🕭

Two heads are better'n one — even if one is a knot-head.

🕭

Absence makes the heart grow fonder — for someone else.

🕭

Mind your Ps and Qs.

🕭

Use a little elbow grease.

🕭

Just give it a lick and a promise.

🕭

Get off your high horse.

There's more than one way
to skin a cat.

Learn or be taught.

They poot in their pants like everybody else.

Mindin' My Manners

Dear Miz Country Manners,
 I was out on a hot date with a sweet li'l gal last weekend and just as I was aimin' to shoot one of the biggest rats I'd ever seen at the dump, I just had to whiz. Of course, bein' the gentleman that I am, I didn't want to use that word in front of Libby Lou Janie Lynn, and I sure didn't want to say something dumb like "tee-tee" or just turn my back and drain my lizard right there in front of her. What should I do? I mean, I really have to go bad now.

Lover Boy

Dear Lover Boy,
 You are right, "tee tee" is a turn-off and mighty inappropriate in the setting you describe. You had several options though. I've listed them below along with other courtesies you might need in the future. If you carry them with you, you can go ahead and let loose at a moment's notice and still be proper.

Miz Country Manners

I'm goin' to water the lily.

☯

I've got to go tap a kidney.

☯

My back teeth are floatin'.

☯

I've got to go shake hands with the bishop.

☯

Your barn door's open and your horse is going to get out. (Your fly's unzipped.)

☯

It's one o clock at the water works. (Your fly's unzipped.)

☯

It's snowin' down south. *(Your slip is showin'.)*

☯

She had an off-white weddin'. (She was pregnant when she got married.)

She's shootin' bunnies. (What children say when some-one toots.)

❂

Just clearin' my throat. (What you say when you break wind.)

❂

Your cough sure does sound better. (What you say to someone else who breaks wind.)

❂

Your voice sounds deeper, but your breath smells the same. (What you say when they break wind again.)

May They Rest in Peace

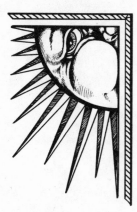 

Remember ol' man Dowdy, the bachelor who'd shoot at my uncle and all his friends when they were kids? Well, there's a little more to that story. Not long after Pencil knocked on his door, Elphus Dowdy passed away. They laid him out in the dining room, like they always did back then, and the parents made those boys dress up and go on over to the Dowdy house to pay their last respects. It was the ultimate humiliation, to be forced to pay homage to someone they despised. And so late on the night before his funeral, when all the friends and relatives were gone and ol' man Dowdy was in that house alone in the only suit he ever owned, the boys snuck in, the one named Hushy leadin' the way. They pulled the ol' coot from his coffin, hoisted him over their heads and hauled him to the beer joint at the bottom of the hill. Then, they smashed in a back window, dragged the bachelor inside, propped him in a corner booth, poured themselves (and him) a drink and toasted him, his buckshot and his gun.

"Here's to ol' man Dowdy," Pencil said. **"And the dirt nap he'll be takin'."**

With that, we say "so long," and offer this selection of adages from the afterlife in the hopes of leavin' you **tickled to death.**

She passed through St. Peter's gate.

🔹

She's been promoted to glory.

🔹

He's pushin' up daisies.

🔹

She's suckin' on daisy roots.

🔹

He's wearing a pine overcoat.

🔹

She's stokin' Lucifer's fires.

🔹

He took the electric cure. (He was sentenced to death.)

🔹

She ran into a bullet.

🔹

He's takin' a dirt nap in the bone orchard.

🔹

Deader'n a doornail.

If they kill 'im, they can't eat 'im.

❂

I wouldn't believe 'im if he was dyin' and knew it.

❂

You're loud enough to wake the dead.

❂

You're dead from the neck up.

❂

You're dead as the dodo.

❂

You're grave smart and life stupid.

❂

You'd screw up a two-car funeral procession.

❂

He was so crooked they had to screw him into the ground to bury him.

❂

If I knew I was goin' to live this long, I would've taken better care of myself.

❂

That would kill 'im deader'n a heart attack.

He's like a graveyard—he'll take anything.

You couldn't satisfy him if you hung him with a new rope.

You could get used to
hangin' if it didn't kill you.